AC
DIS

PUERTO RICANS
From Island to Mainland

PUERTO RICANS
From Island to Mainland

by ARLENE HARRIS KURTIS

Illustrated with photographs

JULIAN MESSNER *NEW YORK*

Published simultaneously in the United States and Canada by
Julian Messner, a division of Simon & Schuster, Inc.,
1 West 39 Street, New York, N.Y. 10018. All rights reserved.

Printed in the United States of America
SBN 671-32084-x Trade
671-32085-8 MCE
Library of Congress Catalog Card No. 69-13128
Design by Marjorie Zaum K.

Photo Credits

Aspira: p. 57
Commonwealth of Puerto Rico, Department of Labor: p. 41, 42, 43, 82
David Corcoran for the Rockland (N.Y.) *Journal-News:* p. 49
East Harlem Tenants' Council: p. 45, 52, 58
Bonnie Freer: p. 84-85
Instituto de Cultura Puertorriqueña: p. 15, 28
Alan A. Kurtis: p. 25, 26, 53, 59
David McAdams: p. 71
New York *Daily News* photo by Mel Finkelstein: p. 62
Carmelo Notijo for *El Diario-La Prensa:* p. 65
Puerto Rico Information Service: p. 12-13, 23, 24, 33, 55, 67, 70, 78-79, 81
United Press International: p. 32, 36, 38, 48, 61

ACKNOWLEDGMENTS

I wish to thank the many people and agencies who were always ready to help in the gathering of material for this book.

Among them are Dr. Ricardo E. Alegriá, Director of the Institute of Culture of Puerto Rico; John Valentin of Aspira; Goddard-Riverside Community Center; Mrs. Edi Quilas of *El Diario-La Prensa;* Peter Bloch, curator of the Alfred Fahndrich Santos collection of the Association for Puerto Rico-Hispanic Culture; the Commonwealth of Puerto Rico, Department of Labor; Mimi Kaprow, Margery Luce, and my husband Alan A. Kurtis who helped in so many ways.

And the students of Junior High School 54 and 99, Manhattan, whom I was privileged to know, and who were the inspiration for this book.

A.H.K.

U. S. 1484936

Contents

PUERTO RICANS
From Island to Mainland

chapter 1.
About 50 B.C. to 1519:
The Land and Its People

"The land of Borinquén where I was born,/Is a flowering garden of magical beauty." These are the first two lines of the national hymn that describe Puerto Rico, a brilliantly green island, smaller than the state of Connecticut, that lies in the Atlantic Ocean a thousand miles from Florida.

The Arawak Indians who came there two thousand years ago from South America would have agreed that it was a fine place to live. They needed little clothing in the warm climate. Because of the bright sun and brief daily rainfall, fruits and grains were plentiful so that there was always enough to eat. The many bays and inlets provided them with fish and shell-food. The tall stalks and grasses made it simple to put together huts for shelter.

The Arawak thrived on this island of plenty they called Borinquén. They had time to discuss tribal affairs in coun-

The hills and mountains of Borinquén were rich in fruits and grains and offered safe hiding places from unwelcome visitors.

13

cil, led by the cacique, or chief. Remains of ball fields have been found throughout the island, proving that there was time for sports, too. Exciting tales were chanted by the storytellers, and the Indians danced in time to the drummer's beat.

On this island of sea and sun there were only two things to fear. One was the wild storms and winds that could twist trees up by the roots. These winds were called hurricanes, after their god of evil, Huracán. They could strike the island any time between August and October.

The other fear was of the Carib Indians from neighboring islands, who were cannibals. The Carib might attack Borinquén at any time, carry off captives and eat them.

November 19, 1493, started off peacefully on the beautiful island. But suddenly an Arawak lookout cried out in alarm. Strange men were climbing onto the beaches! Thinking it was the Carib, the Arawak ran for the hills.

But these strangers were not cannibals. It was an expedition sent out by their Catholic majesties, King Ferdinand and Queen Isabella of Spain. The leader of the expedition was Admiral Christopher Columbus, and this was his second trip to the New World.

When Columbus sailed westward across the Atlantic Ocean from Spain, he was looking for a short route by water to the Indies—China, India and Japan—lands rich in silks and spices. Instead he discovered a group of islands he called the West Indies. One of these islands was Borinquén, which he named San Juan de Bautista, after Saint John the Baptist.

The King and Queen were enthusiastic about the spices,

Breast plate and sword are the mark of the soldier-settler, Ponce de León, Puerto Rico's first governor.

gold and tobacco that Columbus brought from the islands when he returned to Spain. They decided to start a colony on San Juan, the island that was reported to be "the most beautiful and fertile of them all."

Columbus also believed the easygoing Indians could be sold as slaves to the Spaniards. But the Queen objected. She thought of the Indians as her subjects, not as slaves. It was her desire to make them Catholics. Along with the soldier-settlers who would start the colony, the King and Queen sent priests to instruct the natives.

The captain of this expedition was the nobleman Juan Ponce de León. He left Spain in 1508 with a party of fifty men. The next year he was made the first governor of the island.

One of his soldiers was a tall young man we will call

Renaldo Rojas. The adventures that happen to Renaldo, his children and grandchildren could have happened to real people. All the other people mentioned in this book are real and are part of the story of Puerto Rico.

Renaldo took farm animals and tools with him. His family as well as the families of the other settlers would follow later.

Meanwhile, one of their first interests was to find gold, and they told the Indians to lead them to the mines. But the Indians shrugged their shoulders; they didn't know of any such places. The gold in the streams Columbus found did not come from mines. For centuries the running water had washed away thin traces of gold from the rocks and left the pieces in the stream. The King and Queen were disappointed when no rich deposits of gold were found. The settlers' dreams of finding a fortune were ended, too.

When it came to farming, the soldier-settlers also had trouble getting the Indians to help. They refused to work. It was not because they were lazy. The Arawak were used to gathering just as much food as they needed for themselves. When they were forced to work, many ran off to the mountains. Others were killed trying to revolt, or died of diseases brought by the settlers.

"The Indians want to live in their old way," Renaldo Rojas told his governor. "They think of us as friends, not masters."

Ponce de León knew this was true. When he first arrived he had been made a son of the tribal chief as an act of friendship. Now he was feared.

He decided to buy laborers to work in the fields. This

is how a third group of people came to live on the island. Ponce de León received permission from his King to buy Africans from Portuguese slave traders. In 1511 the first boatload of Africans was landed in Puerto Rico to work as slaves.

The King and Queen did not feel the same about these people from Africa as they did about the Arawak Indians. They reasoned that the Africans were subjects of an African king who had traded them to the Portuguese. Therefore Spain was not responsible for them.

These dark-skinned men were strong and learned quickly. But they, too, wanted their freedom. As soon as they could, many of them ran off to the hills and joined the Indians there. Although they fought the soldiers that enslaved them, many had to stay and work the fields. The crops now included sugarcane, which had been brought to the island from Haiti.

The early settlers had other difficulties. The first town, Caparra, had been started on swampy land. Mosquitos from the swamps bit the men, who came down with a disease which we now know was malaria.

In 1519 they left Caparra and began another town, this time on a rocky little island across the bay. This new town they called Puerto Rico, which means "rich port." It was the only port of trade, and people in Spain started to call the whole island Puerto Rico. In a short time it was decided to call the port settlement San Juan, and the whole island Puerto Rico, and that is how it stands today.

Meanwhile, Ponce de León heard that a nearby island contained gold as well as springs and fountains that would cure the men of fevers and make them feel young and strong again. In 1513, he went in search of this Fountain of Youth and discovered Florida.

As for Puerto Rico, despite the early disappointments, it soon proved to have a real value that Spain had not at first imagined.

chapter 2.
1534-1898:
Spain's Most Loyal Colony

"Gold! Gold's been found in Peru!" called the excited ship's captain as he bounded up the steps to the Governor's Palace in San Juan.

The date was 1534, and discouraged Puerto Rican settlers gathered around to hear more about the gold strike.

"If I had not instantly ordered him away," Governor Lando recorded, "the island would have been deserted." He ordered the death penalty for anyone who left the island. Spain wanted the settlers to stay. She needed them to work on ships that stopped in San Juan harbor.

Because of its location, Puerto Rico had become an important military and naval base for Spain. It is one of a chain of islands that make up the Greater and Lesser Antilles. The Greater Antilles are Cuba; the island of Hispaniola, shared by the countries of Haiti and the Dominican

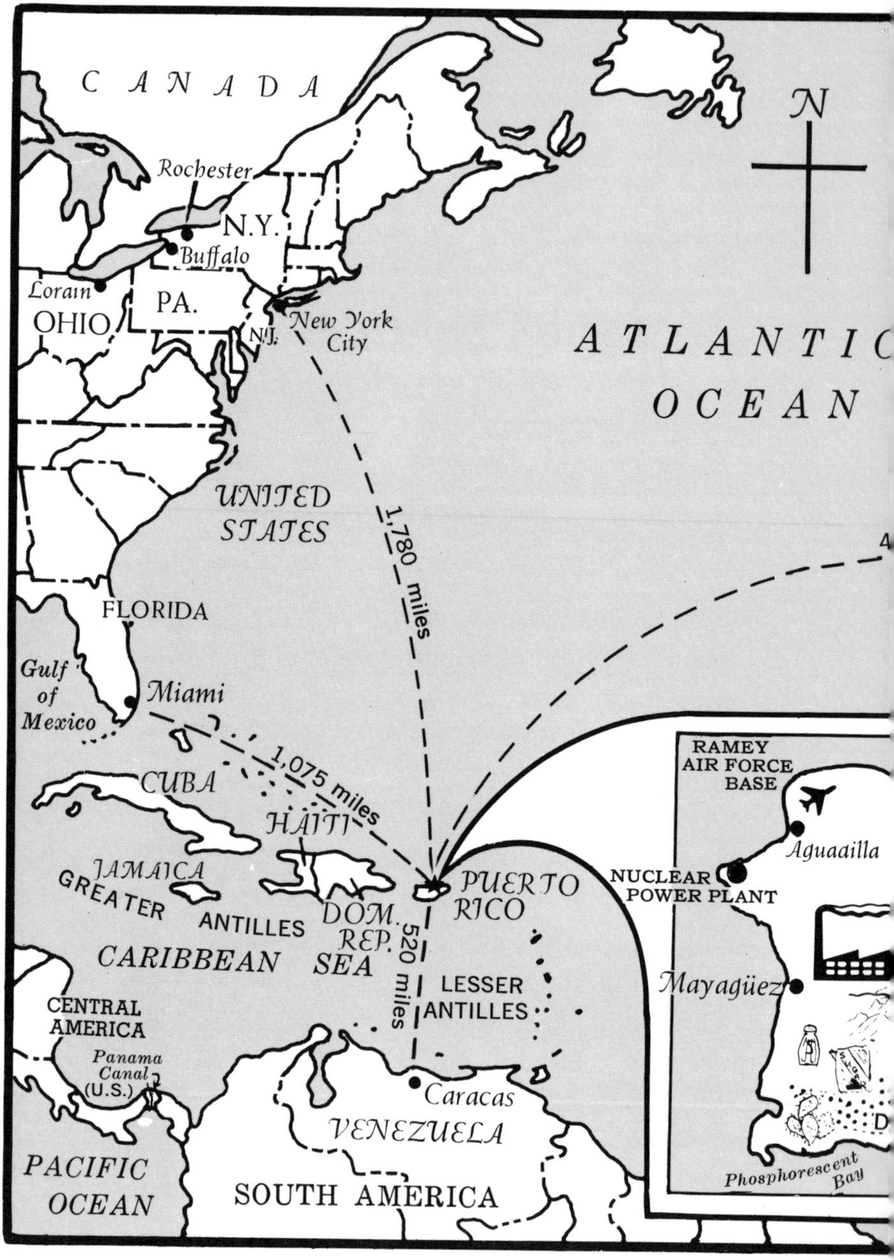

CANADA
N
Rochester
N.Y.
Buffalo
Lorain
PA.
OHIO
N.J.
New York City
ATLANTIC
OCEAN
UNITED STATES
1,780 miles
FLORIDA
Gulf of Mexico
Miami
1,075 miles
CUBA
HAITI
JAMAICA
GREATER ANTILLES
DOM. REP.
PUERTO RICO
520 miles
CARIBBEAN SEA
LESSER ANTILLES
CENTRAL AMERICA
Panama Canal (U.S.)
Caracas
VENEZUELA
PACIFIC OCEAN
SOUTH AMERICA
RAMEY AIR FORCE BASE
Aguaailla
NUCLEAR POWER PLANT
Mayagüez
Phosphorescent Bay

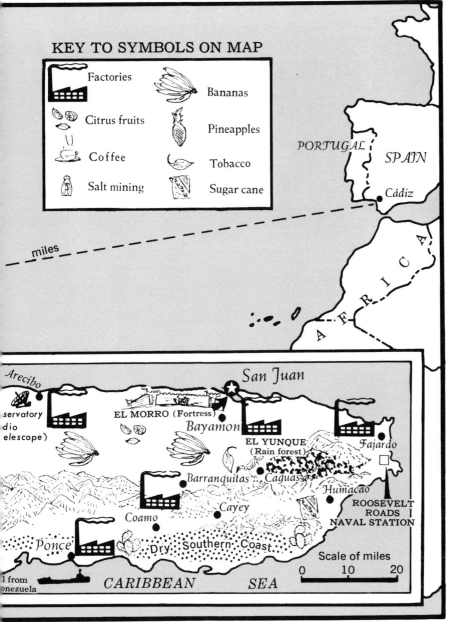

KEY TO SYMBOLS ON MAP

Factories

Bananas

Citrus fruits

Pineapples

Coffee

Tobacco

Salt mining

Sugar cane

miles

PORTUGAL

SPAIN

Cádiz

AFRICA

Arecibo

San Juan

Observatory
(Radio
telescope)

EL MORRO (Fortress)

Bayamon

EL YUNQUE
(Rain forest)

Fajardo

Barranquitas

Caguas

Humacao

Cayey

ROOSEVELT
ROADS
NAVAL STATION

Coamo

Ponce

Dry   Southern   Coast

Scale of miles

0   10   20

Oil from
Venezuela

CARIBBEAN   SEA

Map by William Jaber

Republic; Jamaica; and Puerto Rico. Puerto Rico is the smallest of these four. The Antilles form a rim that fences off that part of the Atlantic Ocean called the Caribbean Sea.

Treasure ships bringing gold from Peru, silver from Mexico, and pearls from Colombia needed a place to stop off for fresh fruit, meat and water before starting out across the Atlantic for Spain. Puerto Rico became a kind of super-service station for Spanish ships going east and west.

Spain knew there was danger to the whole fleet when it was in port at San Juan. The capture of just one ship could make a pirate captain and his crew rich for life. In addition, other nations with colonies in the area looked with envy on the well-located key island. Spain decided she had better build forts to protect Puerto Rico.

Using money taken from her treasury in Mexico, forts were begun along the coast of the island in 1539. One was built on the high rocky tip of San Juan, called El Morro, meaning the headland. Thick stone walls enclosed huge water tanks, ammunition, gun rooms, prisons and soldiers' quarters at five levels.

In 1595 the bold Englishman Sir Francis Drake tried to take the island while a treasure ship was being repaired in the harbor. The first shot from El Morro shattered Drake's cabin, killing one of his officers and wounding another. No matter how Sir Francis steered his ship trying to find a weak spot in the defenses, the fort answered with booming cannon. After three days, Sir Francis Drake and his vessels limped off in defeat.

In later years other Englishmen, the Dutch and French invaded Puerto Rico. But they were never successful in

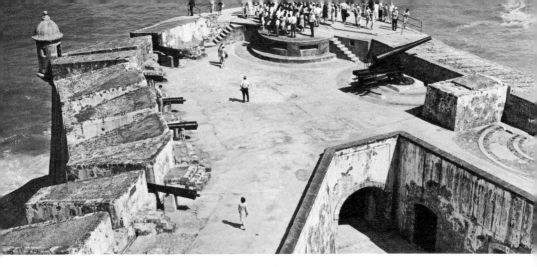

El Morro's guns covered every approach to San Juan. The passageways lead to gun rooms, water tanks, and soldiers' quarters.

taking it, because of the string of forts built around the island and the determined people who fought back.

Despite the loyalty of the islanders, Spain did everything to hamper trade and agriculture. Revolts began in other Spanish-American colonies against this kind of harsh rule. When Mexico rebelled in 1810, the money she contributed to Puerto Rico was cut off. Spain saw that she would have to give the islanders more opportunities to earn money. She invited the colony to send a voting representative to the *Cortes,* the congress of Spain.

Ramón Power Giralt was selected. It is a Spanish custom to add the mother's last name after the last name of the father. This explains why this Puerto Rican is called Ramón Power, but never Ramón Giralt.

Ramón Power was born in 1775. He was a naval officer who preferred to write, and he was an excellent speaker.

Power was so popular at the Cortes of 1810 that he was elected its vice-president. He was able to secure important gains for his island home.

Puerto Ricans could now be appointed to high government posts, instead of being ruled only by Spaniards sent from the mother country. Trade restrictions were lifted, and the island sold sugar, coffee and animal hides to the United States. As a result, agriculture and business got a much needed boost.

The population also climbed. By the early 1800's there were 155,000 people in Puerto Rico. Not only Spaniards came to the island. Frenchmen arrived from nearby Haiti. In 1803 French and Spanish settlers from the United States made their home on the island. That was when President Thomas Jefferson bought Louisiana from the French. The

Tile roofs, shutters, and balconies are all features of a typical Spanish house. Called the "White House," this one was built in San Juan by Ponce de León's children.

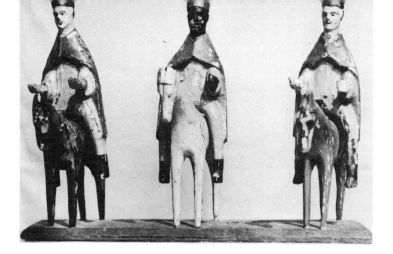

Wood carvers made statues of the saints and painted them with colors made from plant juices. The Three Kings are used in Christmas celebrations.

people from the Louisiana Territory who wanted to live in a Catholic country sailed to Puerto Rico. Irish also came for religious reasons. Even a shipwrecked boatload of Russians scrambled on shore, took a look around the beautiful island, and decided to remain.

All these people were tolerant of each other's differences and lived together in harmony. But since most of the islanders came from a Spanish heritage, the culture was kept alive.

People spoke and wrote in Spanish. They built Spanish-style homes, suited to the tropical climate. The high ceilings and shuttered windows kept the houses cool and airy.

José Campeche, an artist, made his own colors from plants and flowers, and painted on wood beautiful pictures of the saints. Santeros, or wood carvers, in every town made lovely statues of the saints that are prized as treasures today, although at that time they were given away as gifts.

A new apartment house in New York City is named in honor of the Puerto Rican teacher and writer.

Eugenio María de Hostos lived between 1839 and 1903. He was an educator and author whose writing included nursery rhymes as well as plays and essays. Among his many accomplishments was the school system for Santo Domingo, on the island of Hispaniola, which he set up. He was the first Puerto Rican to achieve world fame, and his genius is still acknowledged in Spanish-speaking lands. Today, a new apartment house in New York City has been named in his honor.

Newspapers and books, printed on the island press in the 1800's, were widely read in Spain and South America.

The Spanish culture was kept alive in family life, too.

Whether they lived in the growing cities of the island or in small towns in the hills, all Puerto Ricans belonged to the Catholic church and worshipped in lovely churches or at services held in their homes. If the family could afford the fee, the children went to church-run schools. Wealthy families might send a son to study in one of the old universities in Spain.

Girls were watched over by chaperones until they were

married. No Spanish girl was allowed out of the house without this guardian. The chaperone might be her mother, an aunt, a trusted servant or a married sister. Girls were taught at home. They learned to dance, sew, prepare food, and run a household that would someday reflect honor on their husbands.

No matter whether he was rich or poor, the father was respected as the absolute head of his household. His children followed his orders to the letter. They respected the man for whom their father worked, as a further way of honoring their father. They would feel proud to do errands for anyone in a high position.

This respect and dignity that each Puerto Rican felt toward his superior perhaps explains why the people did not try to revolt with force. Instead, they tried to persuade Spain to grant them more self-government, while declaring their loyalty to her.

In 1866 they asked Spain to give the freed slaves among them the same privileges as other colonists. (When slavery was finally abolished in 1873, only 4 percent of the population were slaves.) But the *Grito de Lares,* a small armed revolt in 1868, failed to gain popular support. Only a few hundred men could be persuaded to take part. However, this revolt gave Puerto Rico its flag.

Secretly, the plotters had had a flag made by three women of the town of Lares. The design included a blue triangle with a star in its center, and three broad red and two white stripes. The flag was raised in the town square.

In 1895 Cuba began its final revolt against Spain. Now Puerto Rico was the last loyal Spanish colony in the Amer-

The triangle is navy blue with a white star, and every other stripe is red. The flag of Puerto Rico was one hundred years old in 1968.

Luis Muñoz Rivera is called the George Washington of Puerto Rico because he was the first elected head of Puerto Rico under Spain.

icas. Seizing on this fact, a Puerto Rican, Luis Muñoz Rivera, a poet turned politician, pressed Spain to grant complete self-rule to the colony.

A Charter of Autonomy (which means self-rule) was granted in 1897, and the jubilant islanders elected their own lawmakers who in turn formed a cabinet or Executive Council. This Council made Luis Muñoz Rivera its premier or chief. Because he was head of this first all-Puerto Rican government, Muñoz Rivera is sometimes called the George Washington of Puerto Rico.

Eight months later, self-rule was struck down. The United States took over, and the island became a colony again.

chapter 3.
1898-1945:
The United States in Puerto Rico

It was hot on the afternoon of July 25, 1898. The whole town of Guánica, on the southwest coast of Puerto Rico, gathered on shore to watch the Americans land. The force of 3,500 was led by General Nelson A. Miles. The soldiers were itchy and steaming in their heavy uniforms that had been issued to them. Some were weak from malaria picked up in Cuba. But they waved to the people watching.

The Puerto Ricans smiled back, and some of them called out "Viva!" (Hurrah!) These islanders and many others hoped that the successful and generous United States would help their country grow. But most important, they hoped the Americans would bring a democratic form of government to their land.

Puerto Rico became part of the United States as a result of the Spanish-American War in which the Americans took Cuba's side in her revolt against Spain. When the war was over, Cuba won her independence, and Puerto Rico along with other territories was ceded, or given, to the United States.

The island's location was a good one for the United States, too. The government was planning to build the Panama Canal between the Caribbean Sea and the Pacific Ocean, as a shortcut. Puerto Rico could guard the entrance from the Atlantic Ocean to the Caribbean Sea. To help protect this whole area, the United States constructed Army and Navy bases, and later an Air Force base, on the island. Roosevelt Roads Naval Base there is the world's largest.

Businessmen were interested in Puerto Rico. Although it had no important natural resources other than its rich soil, crops of sugar, coffee and tobacco could be grown for profit if modern methods were used. Now that Puerto Rico was part of the United States, there would be no duty, or tax, on goods moving back and forth between the island and the mainland. This would mean a bonanza for American manufacturers anxious to sell goods to the islanders and for sugar producers in Puerto Rico, who could now ship sugar into the States duty-free.

Agricultural production soared. A few large companies, one of them French, bought up much of the farmland from small farmers and planted it in sugarcane. Roads were built to speed the cane to mills that shredded the stalks and pressed the juice from the shreds between giant rollers. A coastal railway was built to take the raw sugar to American ships that would transport it to the States. Some of the sugar was made into molasses and rum, which became two of Puerto Rico's important products.

More sugar was produced each year, and the companies

made good profits. But the money was not spent in Puerto Rico. It went out of the country to investors in the United States and France. In a way, these investors were doing the same as Spain had done—taking the resources of the country and giving little in return, for the workers were paid starvation wages.

Samuel Gompers, an American labor leader, reported in 1904, "I have seen men toiling in the sugar fields virtually dragging themselves through fifteen hours a day for forty or forty-five cents."

Manuel Rojas was a cane cutter whose ancestors had come to the island with Ponce de León. But Manuel was a poor man. He lived near Mayagüez, where sugar is grown. The land his family owned had been divided many times among many sons, until the small farm Manuel held had to be sold to pay debts brought on by a season of little rain and poor crops. The large company which bought the farm let Manuel use a small plot, on which he put up a two-room wooden house with a small airless kitchen at the back. In the front was a clear patch of land called a *batey*. In the evening Manuel sat in this front yard talking with friends

Like Manuel, this jíbaro cuts the sugarcane with his sharp machete.

When this field of sugarcane is cut down, these men may be out of work until the next harvest.

or playing dominoes. There was not enough room to raise a garden or keep farm animals, as the family had done when they owned their land.

Before dawn, Manuel rose and left for the fields, wearing the large straw hat called a *pava* and carrying his sharp flat knife, the *machete*. Manuel and his fellow workers stood in the jungle-like growth of sugarcane and slashed at the stalks with swift rhythmic strokes, leaving a short stubble in the ground. At noon, when the sun was high, the men ate lunch brought to them by their wives, napped in the shade, and then returned to work until dusk.

During the "dead season," between June and November, when the cane is growing, there is no work. The cane cutter and his family went hungry. But for the five-month harvest, the families were busy night and day.

These people who worked in the sugar, coffee and tobacco fields in the hills and mountains of Puerto Rico are called *jíbaros*. This is an Indian word that means "those who flee." Their ancestors were the Indians who fled from the Spanish settlers. Later they were joined by Africans who had been freed, as well as those who had escaped. Spaniards also chose to farm the fertile hills and valleys. These three groups had intermarried. They were a tough and independent breed, but poverty was killing them, and worse was yet to come.

A severe hurricane hit the island in 1928. Mrs. Rojas led the children to a shelter Manuel had dug in the ground. She took with her a tin of water and a hand of bananas for food. The oldest daughter carefully carried the *Santos,* the saints carved of wood that the family had kept for generations. The children also wanted to keep safe the statue of the Three Kings that they used at Christmastime.

Eduardo, who was eleven, helped his father hammer boards across the door of the house. Then they rushed into the dugout and fastened the opening.

For three days the wind blew fiercely, up to seventy miles an hour, and the rain fell in heavy drops like hail. The wind was so powerful it could throw a man through the air, cave in a house, uproot a strong tree. Despite the howling of the wind, the family heard something crash on top of their dugout. Then there was a scraping sound as the powerful winds blew away whatever it was that fell.

By the morning of the fourth day, the wind had died down, although it still rained. When Manuel came out of the dugout to check his house, he found the roof was gone.

Buildings lay in ruins all over the island. Not only did

many people lose their lives, but crops were destroyed. The banana trees which shaded coffee bushes were blown down, and as a result the coffee crop was ruined for five years.

Americans rushed food and clothing to the stricken country, which by this time was already called "the poorhouse of the Caribbean." The hungry people lined up as Army trucks rolled into towns and soldiers gave out supplies.

During this period of the 1930's, Americans too were without jobs. Many received money on which to live from the government. It was the time known as the Great Depression.

President Franklin Roosevelt formed agencies to create new jobs in the United States. For the island he started an organization called the Puerto Rico Reconstruction Administration, or PRRA, for short. It began in 1935, and its ideas came from the many Puerto Ricans who were part of the organization. Its main goal was to start industries going so that the island would not be solely dependent on agriculture. At the same time, in a Supreme Court case, the PRRA won the right to buy back land from one of the four large sugar companies. The PRRA formed the sugar workers into a cooperative and, in payment of a small sum, gave each of them a portion of the land to farm.

Shoe factories were started. Hand-embroidered garments were made in workshops and sold in the States, where they were much admired for their beauty. Workers who were taught to sew by machine made underwear and garments of all sorts.

One of the island's few raw materials is limestone, used in the making of cement. A cement plant was built, and the

U. S. 1484936

Hurricane Donna struck Puerto Rico in 1960. It wrecked this house of tin and wood. The concrete home in the background stood up to the fierce winds.

cement produced was made into concrete by adding sand, gravel, and water. The concrete was used to make strong houses whose roofs would not blow off in a hurricane.

These changes meant progress, but they only benefited a small part of the population. However, since the American government had arrived in 1898, other changes had been taking place that affected them all.

One important change was in religion. Catholicism was no longer the only religion on the island. The Protestant church was able to send missionaries and teachers to Puerto Rico. Today 80 percent of the people are Catholic, 15 percent Protestant, and the rest are of other faiths.

Still another change came in education. The University of Puerto Rico was opened in 1903. Today there are five universities on the island.

Free public schools were started, but there were too few

This is the official seal of Puerto Rico. The words on top say "Free Associated State" which is translated "Commonwealth." The lamb means peace and the book stands for wisdom. They are symbols of Saint John the Baptist, for whom Columbus named the island. The Latin words say "John is his name."

Can you guess whose initials are "F" and "I"? The crowns over the letters are a clue that they belong to King Ferdinand and Queen Isabella. The castles, flags, and lions are Spanish symbols of their territories.

classrooms and teachers, and the instruction was in English. In 1947, Spanish once again became the official language in the classroom. Today English is also taught, starting in Grade One.

But the greatest progress took place in government. In 1900 Congress passed the Foraker Act. It provided for the election of a resident commissioner who would live in Washington, D.C., and could speak about island affairs in the House of Representatives but would have no vote. Since the Puerto Ricans could not vote for the President or other national officers, they did not have to pay United States taxes. This is in keeping with the idea of "No taxation without representation" established during the American Revolution. Today this rule still stands—the islanders do not vote for President, and they pay no taxes to support the national government. The present resident commissioner is a young Puerto Rican statesman, Santiago Polanco Abreu.

Under the Foraker Act the islanders were also allowed to elect only one house of their two-house legislature. The President of the United States appointed the members of the other house, as well as the governor, his cabinet and the supreme court judges.

After 1898, Puerto Ricans, of course, were no longer

Side by side. The flag of the Commonwealth flies at the same height as the American flag ever since Constitution Day, July 25th, 1952.

citizens of Spain, but they were not made citizens of the United States until 1917, when the Jones Act was passed. Under this act they could elect all the members of their Legislative Assembly, which now is made up of 32 Senators and 64 Representatives. They meet in San Juan, the capital city, every year in January.

In 1948 the people were at last able to elect their own governor. It was Luis Muñoz Marín, son of the premier under Spanish rule, Luis Muñoz Rivera.

With this step forward, the people wondered about the future status of their land. Should they ask to become a new state in the Union? Would complete independence be better, or was there some other solution? Governor Muñoz put forward another idea. Puerto Ricans would be self-governing in all island affairs, but the United States would handle foreign affairs and defense of the island, just as it does for the states. Puerto Rico would be *almost* a state, but it would not have a vote in the national government nor pay taxes to it.

This arrangement was acceptable to the United States Congress and President Harry S Truman. The Puerto Ricans voted to accept it, too. On July 25, 1952—fifty-four years to the day after United States troops landed—the Commonwealth of Puerto Rico, as it chose to be called, came into being. Every year this occasion is remembered as Constitution Day, because the island's own set of laws went into force at that time.

chapter 4.
1945-1968:
Puerto Ricans in the United States

The silver plane glided smoothly down the runway and came to a stop. A flight of steps was wheeled to the door, which was swung open. Men, women and children began streaming forth. Many of them carried guitars on their back and paper bags or cardboard suitcases in their hands containing their clothes. As they entered the terminal, voices called out from the waiting crowd: "Over here, Pablo!" "This way, María!" "Here, here, Eduardo!" "Welcome, Jíberos!"

It was New York City's LaGuardia Airport and the year was 1945. The greatest migration by air had begun. Almost two million people lived in Puerto Rico, making it the third most densely populated place on earth. A hurricane struck the island that year, too. Jobs were scarce and the future looked bleak. The airlines advertised fares as low as $35 to

New York. Letters from relatives there said, "Come to my city, my boss says he'll give you a job at twice what you're earning now."

So young Puerto Ricans came—13,000 in 1945. Almost 40,000 in 1946!

World War II had ended on September 2, 1945, and New York was humming with activity. There were many jobs that needed doing, and the citizens from Puerto Rico were willing to do them.

During the war, Americans had left unskilled jobs to work in war plants. Now they continued working in factories making peacetime products. There were thousands of openings for unskilled help in service trades. Hotels hired Puerto Ricans as busboys and kitchen helpers. Hospitals needed orderlies and clean-up men. The garment industry, with unfilled orders, was desperate for women who knew how to sew by machine. The Puerto Rican woman had sewing skills, and the manufacturer welcomed her, even if she

After 1945, Puerto Ricans began coming to the United States in large numbers. Passengers board a plane in San Juan for the trip.

Puerto Rican migrants went to work in hotels and restaurants in New York, Boston, Buffalo, and Chicago.

Hospitals needed workers. This X-ray technician was trained on the job in a New York City hospital.

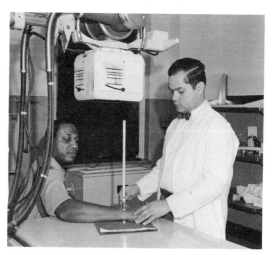

Women skilled in sewing found work in the clothing industry.

had to bring along her little children until she found someone to care for them while she worked.

While most new arrivals settled in New York City, some went to relatives in the Midwest who worked in steel mills. Lorain, Ohio, and Gary, Indiana, put Puerto Ricans to work in iron foundries. New Jersey had places on assembly lines and in canneries. Chicago and Boston received thousands who went to work in service jobs.

These new arrivals were not the first Puerto Ricans to come to the United States. By 1920 Puerto Ricans already lived in every state. Some had come as college students and remained. Others settled in Brooklyn, which they had seen and liked when they were sailors on ships that stopped in New York. Cigar makers from the island had found work in Florida.

Like other immigrants, the Puerto Ricans had to learn a new language. They had to take lower-paying jobs, and so could only afford poor housing.

Mid-west iron and steel plants employed thousands of Puerto Ricans.

But the Puerto Rican was different from the usual immigrant in several ways. He was an American citizen, and so did not come under the new immigration laws that kept foreigners from entering the country. He came by plane, rather than by boat. He stayed in touch with his homeland, even returning more than once for a visit, unlike the immigrants of former times. He came during a period when poor Afro-Americans from the South were arriving in northern cities hoping to find the same improvements he was after. As a result, there were few services set up to help the Puerto Rican become settled.

Eduardo Rojas, the son of the cane cutter Manuel, and his family were among these newcomers. Eduardo worked as a stock clerk in a supermarket and earned $65 a week. He lived in New York City in a part of town called Spanish Harlem or "El Barrio," which means neighborhood. This crowded, run-down area is located between 100th and 125th Street on the east side of Manhattan, one of the city's five boroughs. Here you will see signs and advertisements in Spanish and hear it spoken.

Eduardo, his wife Carmela, and their two-year old son, Roberto, lived in a three-room apartment on the fourth floor of a dingy walk-up building. There was a bedroom with a window that opened into a dark air shaft. The kitchen was crowded. It held a sink from which the enamel had chipped, an old stove that had been scrubbed clean, a yellowed refrigerator that Eduardo had repainted a bright blue, and a small table and chair. Whenever Eduardo came home from work, Carmela served him at this table. As in other Puerto

These tenants point to broken and missing windows and dingy hallways. Over-crowding made bad houses worse.

Rican homes, it isn't the custom for the family to eat together.

The front room, or living room, had a sofa called *el coucho* which was used by friends and relatives who stayed with the Rojas family until they could find a place of their own. A shelf held the *Santos* statues that Carmela had brought from home.

Carmela complained of the cold during the winter in New York. She had never seen snow before. Roberto loved to play in it. But snow also meant a dripping ceiling. They were on the top floor, and the roof leaked when the snow melted. Eduardo had to hold an umbrella over Carmela while she bathed Roberto in the bathroom, to keep the dripping water off him.

One night a rat broke through the plaster. Eduardo rushed out of bed and grabbed a baseball bat. He killed the rat, but after that the family did not sleep well.

45

Despite their miseries, Eduardo and Carmela had hope for the future. Eduardo soon earned $95 a week as manager of the fruit department in the supermarket. He earned even more when he worked overtime. With the money, he bought a record player and later a television set. They were even able to send money home to their parents in Puerto Rico. Now, Eduardo was saving for a down payment on a car, a luxury he never would have dreamed of owning on the island.

Attracted by glowing reports, more Puerto Ricans arrived every year. In 1953, 69,000 Puerto Ricans came to the United States! Such large numbers of new arrivals meant that already existing problems became desperate.

Jobs for unskilled people with little knowledge of English were already taken. The language barrier kept the Puerto Rican from getting jobs where English was necessary, and it also kept him from advancing to better-paying jobs. In school, Spanish-speaking children did not understand what was going on, and many of them dropped out.

Housing was overcrowded to the danger point. In New York City, apartments of four rooms were divided so that except for the kitchen each room housed one family. As many as fifteen people shared one bath and a kitchen. Children waited to wash up at school, and many arrived without breakfast. There was no place for the garbage, so it was tossed out of the window to make room for more. Rats were everywhere. One apartment house on 100th Street, on the west side of Manhattan in New York City, was known as the "Rat Ranch," it was so overrun by rodents.

Cultural differences got in the way of understanding. The newcomers stood in front of buildings until late hours. It was the only relief from the crowded apartment upstairs, but neighbors complained.

When a Puerto Rican woman worked and her husband could not find a job, he felt he had lost his dignity, which is so precious to a father from a Spanish culture. Discouraged, men left their families to try and find work in other cities.

Discrimination because of color added another problem for the dark-skinned Puerto Rican. He was not welcome in certain jobs, hotels or apartment houses, although those with lighter skins were accepted.

In addition, a small group of Puerto Ricans wanted their island to become independent of the United States. They tried to make changes by force. In 1950, an attempt was made to shoot President Harry S Truman. Four years later, a group called the Nationalists fired on congressmen in the House of Representatives in Washington, wounding several members. Puerto Ricans everywhere condemned these persons.

The number of poor people receiving welfare payments rose during this period. Although several members of a family worked, their earnings could not cover the needs of large families. They had to get city aid.

The newly elected governor of Puerto Rico, Luis Muñoz Marín, made some suggestions he thought could help. "Operation Bootstrap" had officially started in 1940, but the war interrupted the plans to bring factories to the island. Now the governor wanted to go full steam ahead so that Puerto Ricans could "pull themselves up by their bootstraps."

In 1948, he sent agents to the United States to talk with businessmen who needed to expand. The agents told them

Operation Bootstrap. The opening of this plant on the island helped Puerto Ricans find year-round jobs. Then they did not have to depend on farming only for employment.

of the advantages of opening factories in Puerto Rico.

"Why should I go there?" asked Mr. Jones, a typical businessman.

"Good climate, lower wages, willing workers whom we will train for you," said the agent.

"Very fine, but I shall have to put up a factory—and that costs money."

"We will build one for you and rent it to you. Also, you will not have to pay taxes to the Puerto Rican government for ten to seventeen years. As you know, you will not have to pay United States taxes either."

This made sense to the businessman, and the wheels of industry started spinning in Puerto Rico; 1,500 factories were opened on the island. They made everything from clothing to pills, from lipstick to parts for television sets.

With United States help, power plants were built to provide electricity for the factories. Roads were paved throughout the island. Slums were cleared and new housing built. Puerto Rico began to hum with activity.

The result was that migration to the United States slowed down. With the promise of a good job, young men chose to stay on the island. In addition, many Puerto Ricans returned home, preferring the warm climate, the lack of discrimination, and the good salary they could now earn there. In 1963, 5,000 more Puerto Ricans returned to the island than came here. As of 1968, about 30,000 come to the States each year, but another 20,000 return home.

These migratory farm workers help plant and harvest crops in New York State during the summer months and return to their families in Puerto Rico when winter comes.

To help people already in the States, the Commonwealth government opened labor offices in Chicago, Boston, Camden (New Jersey), Rochester (New York) and New York City. People could visit the offices to find jobs, housing and help with English. This is the only time in the history of migrations that the home government has followed its people to their new land.

But the Commonwealth didn't stop there. Under contract with the U.S. Department of Labor, each year during the "dead season" farm workers come from the island to help harvest crops in eighteen states. They return to Puerto Rico in time to harvest the sugarcane. In this way they are employed almost year-round, and the United States farmer gets the help he needs.

chapter 5.
Solving Problems Together

There is a Spanish saying, "God helps those who get up early." Puerto Ricans in the United States applied this to themselves by taking an active part in solving their problems.

To deal with housing, tenants' councils were started in the 1950's and 1960's. The East Harlem Tenants' Council, led by young Ted Velez, a social worker, enlisted the help of Puerto Ricans who could speak English to draw up a list of complaints such as no heat on cold days or plaster falling from ceilings and walls. The Council helped distribute booklets such as "You and Your Landlord," printed in English and Spanish, that told tenants of their rights and duties. Together they went to city hall and government hearings to press for better housing.

Carlos Rios, a stocky Puerto Rican who migrated in 1948 and has already served three years in the New York State

A mother points to her broken kitchen ceiling. The Tenants' Council will help see that it is repaired.

Assembly, was elected to the New York City Council in 1966. He led East Harlem residents in protests demanding cleaner streets and more police protection in housing projects.

Reporters of large daily newspapers were taken on tours of the worst slums. Congressman William F. Ryan showed them the "Rat Ranch" on 100th Street. New Yorkers became so enraged when they saw the pictures that the building was torn down. Now a modern twenty-story apartment house for low-income families stands in its place. There are benches in front and in back where people can sit and talk. Across the street are playgrounds, a new library, and a health station. A combined firehouse and police station serves the people of the area.

Voting rights are another serious concern. Once a citizen from the island makes his home in the States, he has the right to vote for all elected officials and, of course, the

President. Yet many Puerto Ricans were denied this right because they could not read English. This seemed unfair to many legislators, since Spanish is Puerto Rico's official language.

In 1965 the Federal Voting Rights Act was passed by Congress. It said that no one with an elementary school diploma, who had been taught in a land under the United States' flag where the classroom language was other than English, could be denied the right to vote.

This new law meant that a person who did not read English could vote, and more and more Puerto Ricans are doing so each year. In New York City, where 70 percent of those who have come to the United States live, they keep up with the news by reading *El Diario—La Prensa* or *El Tiempo,* two Spanish language dailies. They can hear the news on several radio stations or on television's Channel 47, so that even if they do not speak English they can be informed voters.

To find jobs and improve their skills, Puerto Ricans

This twenty-story building, with areas in front and back where people can sit and talk, replaces the "Rat Ranch" on 100th Street in Manhattan, New York City.

The signs on this New York City street say Travel Agency, Grocery Store and Meat Market.

signed up for union programs and work projects started by the United States Office of Economic Opportunity. Employers were paid in part for the cost of training new workers in hospitals, assembly plants and machine shops. Thousands of Puerto Rican young people who had dropped out of school joined the Job Corps in which they could improve their English, get a high school diploma and learn a trade.

Another program helped Puerto Ricans set up their own businesses. Eduardo Rojas and his cousin Papo wanted to start their own grocery store. They went to the Small Business Administration to ask them to back a loan from the bank. They opened a *bodega,* or grocery, on the West Side of Manhattan, where many Puerto Ricans now lived. They stocked it with fruits and vegetables from Puerto Rico, as well as with American products. The *bodega* did a good business, and soon they were able to pay back their loan. Then these funds were loaned to other new businessmen. By 1968, in New York City alone, 5,000 businesses were owned by Puerto Ricans, including 4,000 groceries, many barbershops, small factories and two banks.

Since one of the main reasons for migrating was education for their children, Puerto Rican parents have taken a great interest in how their children do in schools. They tell them to be respectful and neat, but they cannot always help with studies because they may not have gone far in school themselves.

Afternoon class has begun in Roberto Rojas' large class-

A fourth grade class in a Bronx, New York school listens to a classmate's book report. The teacher, Mrs. Carmen Alejandro, was born in Puerto Rico.

room that seats thirty-five fifth graders. A new child enters. He has just moved to Manhattan from Brooklyn.

"Here are my records, Teacher," he says quietly.

Miss Becker smiles. She knows the new boy says "Teacher" with the same respect as he would say "Doctor."

"Hello, Teo," she says, "I am Miss Becker. Class, this is Teo." Then turning to Roberto, she says, "Roberto, please be Teo's buddy this week until he gets settled."

Roberto waves Teo over and makes room for him at the table. Then four more children enter. They do not speak English well. They have been to a special tutoring class where they learn in groups of four. Now it is time for math. The Puerto Rican children in Miss Becker's class are very good in this subject. You do not have to know English to figure, and they have had practice with numbers when they shop for their family.

At two thirty, a pupil by the name of Milagros looks at her watch. The teacher nods to her, and she gets up to go. Milagros leaves early so she can be on time to pick up her brother from kindergarten. She wears a key on a ribbon around her neck. She must not lose it or they will not be able to get into their apartment until their mother comes home from work at six.

So the schools in New York City have learned to help the Puerto Rican youngster. Store-front study halls provide him with a quiet place to do homework after school. Trips taken during school hours help him learn about parts of the city he might otherwise not be able to visit.

But only a small percentage of the Puerto Ricans go on to college. In 1961 an organization called Aspira was

"The meeting is called to order!" Aspira clubs for Puerto Rican teen-agers in New York City offer leadership training and encourage students to "think college."

started to help increase that number. "Aspira" means ambition. And helped by leading Puerto Ricans, American businessmen and the federal government, young Puerto Ricans who want to go to college can now get free language tutoring, financial aid, and guidance.

"I was their first student," Ted Velez, the Tenants' Council director, says warmly. Aspira students are now studying at twenty-six different colleges on full or part scholarships.

To encourage students to "think college," Aspira has formed fifty-two clubs in junior and senior high schools, and other cities are picking up the program. The clubs provide leadership training, and discussion groups help the Puerto Rican to feel pride in his heritage. He has heard how poor and underprivileged he has been for so long; he is down on himself before he starts. Aspira shows him a different

"We'll have the trash ready if you'll come and pick it up," young workers told the Sanitation men. Everyone pitches in during a clean-up drive in East Harlem.

outlook through their art shows and musical events and awards programs. Each year Aspira takes a group of teenagers to Puerto Rico for a tour of the island.

The police have learned how they can help the citizens from Puerto Rico. New York City's 24th Precinct started "Operation Friend." They exchanged visits with Puerto Rican children. Boston police visited Puerto Rico. Patrolmen in Spanish-speaking neighborhoods learned to speak Spanish. The Police Athletic League opened centers at night so that young people could have a place to gather in the evenings and would be less likely to get into trouble. Social workers and policemen help turn gangs into worthwhile clubs. Young men help clean vacant lots and start parks and are encouraged to think of police work for their future careers.

By the 1960's, Puerto Ricans were very much a part of

In New York City, the urge to leave your mark on walls turns into something beautiful. The youngsters of the Goddard-Riverside Community Center painted this mural of city scenes in bright colors.

the life of America. In 1968 New York City had about 800,000 people of Puerto Rican background, more than San Juan. They live in the Morrisania section of the Bronx, throughout Brooklyn and all over Manhattan. There are seventy-two real people named Rojas in the Manhattan telephone book and two pages of Garcias. Including New Jersey cities like Newark and Paterson, there are 1,000,000 Puerto Ricans in what is called Metropolitan New York. The Philadelphia area has about 40,000, and Chicago has about 80,000. Altogether about 1,300,000 Puerto Ricans live in the United States, including Hawaii and Alaska.

These people are making strides. They know there is much to be done, but they also have proven, as the Spanish proverb puts it, "Three helping each other can bear the burden of six."

chapter 6.
We Learn from Each Other

President Johnson said in a speech in 1964:

"Our object is not to make all people alike. It is, as it has always been, to allow ready access to every blessing of liberty, while permitting each to keep his sense of identity with a culture and tradition of his own."

There are Puerto Rican communities in every major city of the United States. They have a special flavor which enriches American life. Let's visit a Spanish-American grocery, like Eduardo's, and see what we can discover.

There are shelves of American products, but the vegetable bins are piled with some Puerto Rican favorites like huge gnarled yams. Another bin holds large green bananas, called plantains. These must be cooked to be eaten and take the place of potatoes in some recipes. The green banana leaves are used to wrap dumplings. They give the filling inside a rich flavor, but are not themselves eaten.

Oval yellow speckled fruit, called mangos, have a sweet taste and are used in salads and for dessert.

The store is quiet because it is noontime, and people are either at work or eating lunch. It will be busy later in the evening, but one young mother is there with her two children. She buys a sugared yam slice for five cents for her little girl. She smiles and nods her head "yes" when her son pulls a bag of plantain chips, like potato chips, from the rack. In her cart she also has a tin of guava paste that she will serve with a white cheese for dessert. Her wagon has three large cans of fruit juice, a large bottle of oil, and two ten-pound sacks of rice and beans. Although rice and

This is a market in Spanish Harlem. Dried beef and salt pork are stacked on the counter above the huge bags of rice and beans.

beans are not grown on the island, they are eaten almost every day because of their low cost.

Dried codfish and salt pork, which do not require refrigeration, are stacked on the counter in the *bodega.* For fresh meat, one would go to the *carnecería,* or meat store, where chicken and pork are most popular. In the *repostería,* or bakery, fresh bread and cakes are sold.

That evening, in this West Side neighborhood in Manhattan, a concert is held in Riverside Park. It is summer, and a thousand people are sitting on blankets on the sloping lawn and listening to a symphony orchestra. The members of the orchestra sit on a stage which is really a truck with one side lowered, called a show-mobile. A well-known soprano, Graciela Rivera, who has sung with the Metro-

On Manhattan's Lower East Side a pig is roasted to celebrate the start of a new playground. In the town squares of Puerto Rico, pigs are barbecued and the juicy slices sold to on-lookers. Pig-on-the-spit is called léchon asado.

Graciela Rivera sings Puerto Rican songs as well as opera. With the Julito Rodriguez Trio, she performed at Radio City Music Hall.

politan Opera, will present some Spanish and Puerto Rican music.

She explains that she will sing one of Rafael Hernandez's songs of the jíbaro, and everyone sighs. Rafael Hernandez is a Puerto Rican hero because he composed beautiful songs about his island that are favorites throughout Latin America. He died in 1963 and a statue in his honor will be erected on the island.

Puerto Rican music is played with guitars, bongos and maracas. There is no better example of the blending of cultures than in music. The *bongos,* or small drums, come from the Africans. The *maracas,* or gourds filled with seeds, are from the Indians. The thin four-stringed *cuatro* is like the Spanish guitar.

A popular form of Puerto Rican music is the *danza,*

slow and romantic and good for dancing. The Puerto Rican anthem, "La Borinqueña," was originally a danza, but now it is played faster, like a march. This is a translation of the words of the song:

LA BORINQUÉÑA
(Hymn to the Land of Borinquén)

The land of Borinquén where I was born,
Is a flowering garden of magical beauty.
The sky, always bright, is an overhead canopy,
And the waves at your feet play a soft lullaby.

When Columbus landed on your beaches,
He exclaimed, full of wonder . . .
Oh, Oh, this is a most beautiful land I have found,
This island of Borinquén, this island of sea and sun,
Of sea and sun, of sea and sun.

A ten-line song, made up about an important event, is called a *decima,* because "dec" means ten. The *plena,* Puerto Rico's own invention, is a song about love, or a local happening that affects one's feelings. Christmas and holiday songs are called *aguinaldos.*

The Puerto Rican's love of music is matched by his love of sports. Baseball is the favorite. On the island, each large city has a professional team. The top teams plays teams from other countries in the Caribbean. The baseball season runs from October to February, and this allows major league players from the States to play winter ball on Puerto Rican teams. The island's Little Leagues have produced

Baseball is a favorite sport for Puerto Ricans here and on the island. These Little Leaguers are about to battle each other in New York City's Central Park.

many major league ballplayers. In the United States, Puerto Ricans often go to baseball games and help form Little League teams which their youngsters hope to join as soon as they can swing a bat.

Kite flying is popular now that it has been brought here from Puerto Rico where the breeze-swept beaches make it a natural sport. Puerto Ricans follow boxing and wrestling matches with enthusiasm, and they groaned when Carlos Ortiz, a Puerto Rican, lost the lightweight crown in 1968 that he had held for two years. Fishing is a sport as well as an industry in Puerto Rico. At dawn in seaport cities of the United States, you will find many Puerto Ricans ready to board a fishing boat on their day off. Cockfights, popular on the island, are not allowed in the States.

Holidays and celebrations are best when shared, and the citizens from Puerto Rico prove this with their Puerto Rican Day Parade in June in New York. Thousands march up Fifth Avenue, and gay floats tell the story of the island. Youth groups sing and dance and sprinkle flowers as they go by. Towns in Puerto Rico send their officials and bands to take part in the march. There are over seventy clubs in the New York area, each one representing a Puerto Rican hometown, and their members join in the parade. In 1968 there were similar parades in New Jersey and Connecticut.

Puerto Rican Discovery Day is celebrated on November 19. Christmas is saved for Three Kings Day, which falls on January 6. The night before, children put down a path of grass or hay, leading under their beds. They hope the camels or horses on which the Kings ride will eat the hay and leave a gift. Today, children of Puerto Rican background in the United States also wish to celebrate Christmas on December 25 as well as January 6. Of course, this means a double serving of gifts. San Juan Day is celebrated in June in honor of the saint for whom the island was originally named.

Horns are tooting, white streamers are flying, as a group of cars go by. Look inside, you will see a bride! Saturday weddings are big events, and the family and friends of the bride and groom want to share their joy with everyone.

Puerto Ricans place great value on family life, and this

is another of their contributions. All members of a family remain close throughout their lives. They are always ready to take in another relative or bring up a child of a friend or relative, no matter how poor they themselves may be. In addition to natural parents and god parents, aunts, uncles and cousins, Puerto Rican children have co-parents. The co-parents are close friends who take special interest in the child and feel honored to have this role. Feeling loved by so many people makes the Puerto Rican boy and girl feel safe.

If he is truly to retain his own culture, the Puerto Rican

Three Kings Day pageant in Puerto Rico is held on January 6th. One "King" stands in the center over a small straw manger scene. The boy on right wears a pava with his shepherd's costume.

will want to continue speaking Spanish. But won't this hold back his advancement in an English-speaking land? The answer has two parts.

The young Puerto Rican learns English for work and community activities. At home and in his clubs he enjoys speaking Spanish. The older citizens do not learn so fast, and this has had surprising results. Americans who work with Spanish-speaking people—social workers, teachers and salesmen—have begun to learn Spanish. Students, knowing that they can really use the language in travel or even in their hometown, have a greater interest in mastering it.

Thanks to our Puerto Rican and other Spanish-speaking citizens, the United States is fast becoming a bilingual country. This benefits the nation in its dealings with South America and Spain, and in making visitors from these lands feel more at home when they visit the United States.

Another important contribution of the citizens from Puerto Rico is their color blindness. This means they take little notice of differences in skin color. Poverty and lack of education—not his color—have kept the black Puerto Rican from rising to the highest levels in island affairs. But as conditions for learning and working improve, so will his role. Puerto Rican families and friendship groups in the United States may contain light- and dark-skinned members, but all are equally loved. At a time when the United States is striving for all people to live together in peace, Puerto Ricans who have been doing it for centuries point the way.

chapter 7.
Heroes and Heroines of Today

Puerto Rico has contributed some of our most outstanding citizens who live and work in the U.S.A. and on the island. Among the most brilliant is the island's first elected governor, Luis Muñoz Marín.

Grandson of the town mayor of Barranquitas and son of Puerto Rico's first premier, Luis Muñoz Marín was born on February 18, 1898, just ten days after his father took office under the Charter of Autonomy. Luis Muñoz Marín lived in New York City and attended P.S. 87. When he was twelve his father became resident commissioner, so Luis lived in Washington, D.C., and later graduated from Georgetown University there. He returned to Puerto Rico to work on the newspaper that his father founded, and then was elected a senator in the Puerto Rican legislature. He stirred the jíbaros into realizing that by their votes they could elect representatives who would fight for their inter-

Luis Muñoz Marín, the first elected governor, was a good friend of President John F. Kennedy.

ests. They responded by making Muñoz governor in 1948 and for three terms thereafter. The big man with the ready smile started Operation Bootstrap and later Operation Serenity, aimed at developing the islanders' talents in the arts. In 1964, he felt it was time to make way for new leaders, and he backed his aide for governor. Now Luis Muñoz Marín is a senator once more.

The second elected governor, Roberto Sánchez Vilella, is a tall powerfully built man who was born in 1913 in Mayagüez, now Puerto Rico's third largest city. Governor Sánchez went to high school in Ponce, Puerto Rico's second largest city, and then studied engineering at Ohio State University. He entered government service and was elected governor in 1964.

In 1968, the Puerto Ricans elected Luis Ferré governor

in a close three-way race. Born in Ponce in 1904, the new governor is a spry business leader who favors eventual statehood for the island.

Known as "the fighting admiral" for his battle victories in the South Pacific during World War II when he was gunnery officer on the battleship *San Juan,* Admiral Horacio Rivero, Jr., is another outstanding Puerto Rican. He was born in Ponce in 1910, graduated third in his class at the U.S. Naval Academy and is now Commander-in-Chief of the Allied Forces in southern Europe.

Most people in the United States of Puerto Rican background are young, but many have already risen to places of importance in state and city governments. They serve as judges, commissioners and representatives in state legislatures.

Slim and vivacious, Miss Josephine Nieves, who was born

Josephine Nieves is the Northeastern Director of the U.S. Office of Economic Opportunity.

Roberto Sánchez Vilella was elected governor in 1964 for a four-year term. Puerto Rican youngsters wear their school uniforms when they visit his office.

Herman Badillo is the Borough President of the Bronx.

José Ferrer, actor, producer, and singer.

in New York City, but whose parents came from Puerto Rico, is "the boss" to two hundred staff workers in the Northeastern District of the Office of Economic Opportunity. After graduation from the City College of New York, this young social worker was an organizer for a lower East Side community center in the city and for the Neighborhood House in Lorain, Ohio, where many Puerto Ricans have settled. Now she helps advise and provide financial aid to community projects like Head Start and work programs in New York, New Jersey and all of New England, the only woman to hold this high position.

The outspoken president of the Borough of the Bronx in New York City is Herman Badillo. He was born in Caguas, Puerto Rico, in 1929. He went to City College in New York and Brooklyn Law School, where he led his class. As Commissioner of Relocation, he was fearless in doing battle with every government agency to see that people who had to move because of slum clearance were fairly treated. He has been a busy borough president since 1966, but he has time for community parties and to meet with the people of his borough, which has a huge Puerto Rican population.

In the field of the arts and sports Puerto Ricans are also well represented.

José Ferrer, actor, director and producer, was born in 1912 in Santurce, a part of San Juan. After graduation from Princeton University, he began an outstanding stage

Orlando Cepeda of the St. Louis Cardinals.

and movie career. He had won an Academy Award for his role in the movie *Cyrano de Bergerac* in 1950, and he starred in *Man of La Mancha* in 1967 on Broadway. Mr. Ferrer is on the Board of Governors of Aspira and is active in helping young performers.

Justino Díaz is a leading basso with the Metropolitan Opera. Jesús María Sanromá is a concert pianist with the Boston Symphony, and Tito Puente is a popular orchestra leader. Of course, one of the outstanding musicians in the world is cellist Pablo Casals. Although born in Spain of a Puerto Rican mother, Casals chose to make his home in Puerto Rico where he is the guiding light of the fine symphony orchestra there.

Piri Thomas is the author of a 1968 best-selling book, *Down These Mean Streets.* Born in East Harlem of parents who came from the island, his book tells about the anger and sorrow of a boy growing up in East Harlem, and what he did about it.

In the field of sports, professional baseball teams are studded with stars who were born in Puerto Rico. Roberto Clemente, of the Pittsburgh Pirates, was voted the National League's Most Valuable Player in 1967 and has been batting champion for four years. Orlando Cepeda plays for the 1967 World Series champion St. Louis Cardinals and is the only National League players ever to be chosen unanimously as Most Valuable Player. He plays winter ball in Puerto Rico and coaches Little League teams.

Charles Pasarell, also born in Puerto Rico, was the United States Intercollegiate Tennis Champion while at the University of California. He is the top-ranking amateur from the United States.

chapter 8.
Looking Forward

In 1967 the people of the island voted on whether or not to continue as a commonwealth. They streamed down the hills and lined up in the cities to cast their ballots. Their answer was "yes," 60 percent voting to continue, 39 percent preferring to apply for statehood, and 1 percent wishing to cut off ties with the United States.

The Commonwealth of Puerto Rico has come a long way since it was called the "poorhouse." It has dragged its way up the steep path from the help*less*ness of the 1920's to the help*ful*ness of the present. Now it is Puerto Rico who gives advice to underdeveloped countries. Puerto Rico today is unique, and part of its special character is the contrast between new and old.

A modern atomic reactor at Rincón, on the northwest coast, produces electricity for the island; yet some mountain people still use kerosene lamps to light their huts. Although

Modern hotels and tall apartment houses tower above the ocean in the modern capital city of San Juan.

the Defense Department maintains the Arecibo Ionospheric Observatory in a natural bowl created by a valley, where radar has already bounced signals off Venus, there are hills and valleys that stay the same as they have for centuries. El Yunque, located in the Caribbean National Forest and the only tropical forest in the United States park system, measures twenty-five feet of rain each year, yet there are parts on the southern coast of the island that are so dry, cactus grows. While the government promotes the building of skyscraper hotels and houses, it also preserves Old San Juan and is restoring Ponce de León's original settlement of Caparra.

Puerto Rico's income is one of the fastest growing in the world. Yet thirteen out of one hundred workers cannot find a job. The number may go higher as wages are raised to United States levels, and businessmen who have used up their tax-free ten years, decide to leave the island. To balance this, the government is trying to attract more steel plants and oil refineries to make products from crude oil imported from nearby Venezuela.

The 1965 estimate of 2,700,000 people on the island is expected to reach 3,000,000 by the census of 1970. San Juan, the capital, has a population of 600,000 alone. Because half the people work in industry, rather than in agriculture, the government spends 35 cents of every tax dollar for education so that young people will learn needed skills.

The products turned out by the more than 2,500 manufacturing plants brought in by Operation Bootstrap include textiles and clothes, electrical equipment, plastics and chemicals. Puerto Rico makes enough shoes each year for every

The Arecibo Ionospheric Observatory is the largest in the world. It fills a natural hollow in these limestone hills.

Ferns are 70 feet tall and the rainfall measures 25 feet a year in the Luquillo National Forest. The forest is called El Yunque (the anvil) for the rock at its very top.

family in the United States to buy one pair. The island is the fifth biggest customer of the United States and in turn sends to the mainland most of its exports.

Agriculture is the second largest source of income. The island is determined to feed itself and not depend on imported food. As a result dairying has become the most important agricultural activity, followed by animal raising. Sugar now ranks third and is confined to the fertile northern coastal plain. Other crops are tobacco, coffee, pineapples, coconuts and other fruits and vegetables.

The third most important industry is tourism. About half a million visitors fly to the island each year. Some are Puerto Ricans from the United States visiting relatives. Others are businessmen, looking after their investments and considering new ones. But most are visitors on holiday, fleeing the biting cold of northern winters, and choosing the paradise island because of its perfect climate, quiet beaches, historical sightseeing and luxurious hotels.

In the United States, the story of the Puerto Rican migrant is still in the making. More and more people of Puerto Rican birth or background have found a place for themselves in almost every field, and the families earning over $10,000 a year are increasing rapidly. But the numbers needing welfare payment to live are growing, too.

Problems continue, but by making himself heard, the Puerto Rican is stimulating answers. Answers to big questions like how to cure poverty and improve housing and education. When the answers are found they will benefit everyone.

In the United States the Afro-American outnumbers the

Puerto Rican twenty to one. But instead of competing with him for jobs and housing, the Puerto Rican is joining with him in constructive efforts to press demands for better opportunities to serve the community as court officials, law officers and educators.

To the hustle and bustle of twentieth-century American life, with its citizens of Asian, African and European backgrounds, add the citizen from Puerto Rico, who is a blend himself of three groups. He can cement understanding between the black and white community because he embraces them both. The story of Puerto Ricans from island to mainland is still in the making, and all Americans today are part of it.

Pronunciation Guide and Glossary

One out of twenty of the world's people speak Spanish, but pronunciation can vary from one country to another. This guide uses the Puerto Rican pronunciation, but even on the island exact sounds vary from city to city.

However, all Spanish-speaking people agree that when a word starts with an "R" it is trilled. To trill, say "R" but vibrate your tongue while doing so. Say PWER-toh RREE-koh for Puerto Rico.

Proper Nouns

Antilles	an-TEE-yas	a chain of islands in the West Indies
Arawak	AH-rah-wahk	the ancient Indians of Puerto Rico
Arecibo	ah-re-SEE-boh	city where observatory is located
Aspira	ah-SPEE-rah	Puerto Rican organization
Badillo, Herman	bah-DEE-yoh, HER-man	Bronx Borough President
Barranquitas	bah-ran-KEY-tas	mountain town
Borinquén	boh-reen-KEN	Indian name for Puerto Rico
Cacique	KA-see-kay	Arawak council leader
Campeche, José	kahm-PAY-chay, hoh-SAY	Artist
Caparra	kah-PAH-rah	First settlement

88

Carib	KAH-rib	West Indian tribe
Caribbean Sea	kari-BEE-an	part of the Atlantic Ocean
Cepeda, Orlando	say-PAY-dah, ohr-LAHN-doh	baseball player
Clemente, Roberto	klay-MEN-tay, roh-BAIR-toh	baseball player
Cortes	KOR-tes	Congress of Spain
Díaz, Justino	DEE-as, hoos-TEE-noh	singer
El Diario-La Prensa	el-dee-AHR-ee-oh la-PREN-sah	Spanish-language newspaper in New York City
El Morro	el-MOR-roh	fort at the tip of San Juan
El Tiempo	el-tee-EM-poh	Spanish-language newspaper in New York City
El Yunque	el-YOON-kay	tropical forest
Ferré, Luis	fer-RAY, loo-EES	leading businessman and governor-elect, 1968
Ferrer, José	fer-RER, hoh-SAY	actor, producer, director
Guánica	gwah-NEE-kah	town where U.S. troops landed in 1898
Hernández, Rafael	air-NAN-des, rah-fy-EL	composer
Hispaniola	iss-pan-YOH-lah	island shared by Haiti and the Dominican Republic
"La Borinqueña"	lah-bohr-in-KEE-nyah	national song
Lares, Grito de	LAR-ess, GREE-toh day	revolt of 1868 in Lares
María de Hostos, Eugenio	ma-REE-ah day OSS-tos, ay-oo-HE-nee-oh	educator
María Sanromá, Jesús	ma-REE-ah sahn-ro-MAH, hay-SOO	pianist
Mayagüez	mah-yah-GWES	third largest city
Milagros	me-LAH-gross	girl's name
Muñoz Marín, Luis	moon-YOHS mah-REEN, loo-EES	first elected governor

Muñoz Rivera, Luis	moon-YOHS ree-VAY-rah, loo-EES	premier under Spain
Nieves, Josephine	NYEH-ves, Josephine	Northeastern Director Office of Economic Opportunity
Ortiz, Carlos	or-TEES, KAR-los	boxing champion
Pasarell, Charles	pah-sah-REL, Charles	tennis champion
Polanco Abreu, Santiago	poh-LAN-koh ah-BRAY-oo, san-tee-AH-goh	Resident Commissioner
Ponce	PON-say	second largest city
Ponce de León, Juan	PON-say day lay-OHN, WHAHN	first governor
Power Giralt, Ramón	pow-AIR hee-RAHLT, rah-MOHN	first representative to the Cortes
Puerto Rico	PWER-toh RREE-koh	first the name of the port, then the island
Rincón	reen-KOHN	city where atomic reactor is located
Rios, Carlos	REE-oss, KAR-lohs	New York City councilman
Rivera, Graciela	ree-VAY-rah, grah-see-EL-ah	singer
Rivero, Horacio	ree-VAY-roh, oh-RAY-see-oh	Admiral, U.S. Navy
Rojas, Carmela	RO-hahs, kar-MEL-ah	
——— Eduardo	——— ed-WAHR-doh	
——— Manuel	——— MAN-yoo-el	⎱ imaginary people in
——— Papo	——— PAH-poh	this book
——— Renaldo	——— ray-NAHL-doh	
——— Roberto	——— roh-BAIR-toh	
San Juan	san-WHAHN	capital and largest city
Sánchez Vilella, Roberto	SAHN-chez vee-LAY-yah, roh-BAIR-toh	Governor 1964
Teo	TAY-oh	boy's name
Velez, Ted	VEE-les, Ted	Director of East Harlem Tenants' Council

Spanish Words

aguinaldo	ah-gee-NAHL-doh	Christmas song
batey	bah-TAY	front yard
bodega	boh-DAY-gah	grocery store
carnecería	kar-nes-sah-REE-ah	butcher shop
cuatro	KWA-troh	four-stringed guitar
danza	DAN-sa	slow song
décima	DES-ee-mah	ten-line song
el barrio	el-BAH-ree-oh	the neighborhood; also Spanish Harlem
jíbaro	HEE-bah-roh	countryman, mountain dweller
lechón asado	lay-CHON ah-SAH-doh	roast pig
machete	mah-SHEH-tay	sharp knife for cutting sugarcane
mango	MAN-goh	a fruit
maracas	mah-RAH-kahs	gourd rattles
pava	PAH-vah	large straw hat
plantain	PLAN-tayn	banana-like fruit
plena	PLAY-nah	song of emotion
repostería	ray-poss-teh-REE-ah	bakery
santeros	sahn-TEE-rohs	wood carvers of saints
santo	SAN-toh	saint, carved statue
viva!	VEE-vah	hurrah!

Index

95